The Strange Case of
Dr Jekyll & Mr Hyde

by Robert Louis Stevenson

Retold by Dennis Hamley

Series Editors: Steve Barlow and Steve Skidmore

Published by Heinemann Educational Publishers
Halley Court, Jordan Hill, Oxford OX2 8EJ
A division of Reed Educational and Professional Publishing Ltd

OXFORD   MELBOURNE   AUCKLAND
JOHANNESBURG   BLANTYRE   GABORONE
IBADAN   PORTSMOUTH NH (USA)   CHICAGO

05   04   03   02   01
10   9   8   7   6   5   4   3   2   1
ISBN 0 435 21338 5

Illustrations by Mike White
Cover design by Shireen Nathoo Design
Cover artwork by Paul Young
Designed by Artistix, Thame, Oxon
Printed and bound in Great Britain by Athenaeum Press Ltd

Tel: 01865 888058   www.heinemann.co.uk

Contents

Characters

Mr Utterson is a
lawyer in London.
Everybody respects
him.

Dr Lanyon is a
doctor in London.

Dr Jekyll is a doctor
who is famous for
his scientific
experiments.

Richard Enfield is Mr Utterson's cousin. He goes to lots of parties. He enjoys the night-life in London.

Poole is Dr Jekyll's butler.

Edward Hyde is a strange and unusual man.

CHAPTER 1

The door in the wall

One Sunday morning, Mr Utterson was taking a walk with his young cousin, Richard Enfield. They turned down a side street.

'Do you see that door?' said Richard.

The door was drab and dirty. It was set in a blank wall with no windows.

'Something unpleasant happened here not long ago,' said Richard. 'I saw it when I was walking home from a party. I cannot forget it.'

'Tell me about it,' said Utterson.

'It was past midnight,' said Richard.
'A little girl came out of a nearby house.
She was on her way to fetch a doctor.

'Suddenly, a man ran round the corner.
He knocked the girl down. Then he raised
his stick as if he was going to smash her
head in. I shouted at him and he ran away.
I ran after him and caught him. I said
I would call the police.

'The man was small with an evil face.

'Everyone was angry, but the man did not care. He said his name was Edward Hyde. He was willing to pay any sum of money to the girl's parents. In return, we were to say nothing to anyone about what had happened.

'I thought I would ask for a lot of money. "£100," I said. "Done," he answered. He took out a key and opened this door. Then he went inside and came out with a cheque.

' "That should keep you quiet," he said.'

'Did you take it?' asked Utterson.

'Of course,' said Richard. 'It was signed by one of the most famous names in London.' He took a cheque from his pocket and showed it to his friend.

Mr Utterson was worried. He knew the

name on the cheque. It was Dr Jekyll.

Dr Jekyll was famous for his experiments in science. Mr Utterson was Dr Jekyll's lawyer. They were old friends.

When Mr Utterson came home, he took Dr Jekyll's will out of his safe. Part of the will said: 'If I should die or disappear, Mr Edward Hyde must have everything I own.'

Until that day, Utterson had heard nothing else about Edward Hyde. Why should Dr Jekyll have such a horrible friend?

Mr Utterson thought of an answer. 'Blackmail,' he said. 'Who is this Mr Hyde?'

CHAPTER 2

Hyde is found

Mr Utterson went to see his friend,
Dr Lanyon.

'Have you seen Jekyll lately?' he asked.

'I have not seen him since he told me
his new ideas,' said Dr Lanyon. 'He thinks
that there are two separate people inside
every human being.'

'Do you know a friend of Jekyll's –
Mr Edward Hyde?'

'I have never heard of him,' said
Dr Lanyon.

Mr Utterson knew he had to find

Hyde. 'If you are Mr Hyde, I am Mr Seek,'
he said to himself.

That night, Mr Utterson waited outside
the door in the wall. The street was quiet.
He watched for hours, but he saw nobody.

Utterson was there again the next
night and the night after that. There was
no sign of Hyde. On the fourth night, the
weather was fine and frosty. Utterson heard
footsteps. A dark shape was coming along
the street.

Utterson saw the shape was a man.
He suddenly felt frightened. There was
something evil about this man. He stopped
by the door. He took out a key. Mr Utterson
stepped out of the shadows.

'Mr Hyde, I think,' he said.

'You are correct. My name is Edward Hyde. Who are you?' answered the man.

'A friend of Dr Jekyll.'

'Dr Jekyll is not at home,' Hyde answered. 'How do you know me?'

'Before I tell you that, let me see your face,' said Utterson.

Hyde turned to him. Mr Utterson gasped. Hyde looked so evil, but Utterson could not say why.

'I will give you my address,' said Hyde. He gave him the number of a house in a seedy part of London. 'Now, tell me how you know me.'

'Dr Jekyll told me about you.'

'You lie,' Hyde snarled. He went inside and slammed the door behind him.

Mr Utterson walked on. He stopped in front of a house. This house was large and looked very pleasant. Dr Jekyll lived there.

Mr Utterson rang the doorbell. The door was opened by a butler.

'Good evening, Poole,' said Utterson. 'Is Doctor Jekyll at home?'

'I will see, sir,' Poole answered.

Utterson waited inside by the fire. Soon Poole returned. 'I'm afraid not, sir,' he said.

'I saw Mr Hyde go in through the back door to the laboratory,' said Utterson.

'Yes, sir. Mr Hyde comes here sometimes,' Poole replied.

'I believe something strange may be happening to Dr Jekyll,' Utterson said.

CHAPTER 3

A shocking murder

Dr Jekyll invited Mr Utterson to dinner. They had a pleasant meal. Then Utterson asked him about Hyde.

Dr Jekyll looked frightened. 'I cannot tell you what is happening,' he said. 'All I can say is that I shall never be rid of Hyde. When I am gone, you must see that poor Hyde gets his rights.'

A few days later, everyone in London was shocked by a terrible murder.

MORNING POST

November 15, 1884

MIDNIGHT MURDER

A man was murdered last night at midnight. The murder was seen by a maid from a nearby house. She noticed 'a nice old gentleman' walking along the street.

Suddenly, another man jumped out of a doorway and started to hit him with a stick. He clubbed the old gentleman to the ground and kept hitting him until he was dead.

The maid fainted. She did not recover for two hours. Then she called the police. 'I know the man who did it,' she said. 'He has visited this house. His name is Edward Hyde.'

The police found a heavy stick near the body. They think the man was killed with it.

The police did not know who the dead man was. They found a letter addressed to Mr Utterson on his body. So they called at Utterson's house.

Then they took him to the police station to see the body. 'This is Sir Danvers Carew, Member of Parliament,' he said. 'I am his lawyer. Who would kill such a good man?'

'Edward Hyde,' said the police inspector.

'His name is on this stick. It was used to kill Sir Danvers Carew.'

Mr Utterson knew the stick. He had given it to Dr Jekyll many years ago. It was a present.

'I have Mr Hyde's address,' he said.

'Then we will go there at once,' said the police inspector.

They stopped outside a shabby house. An old lady opened the door.

'Mr Hyde is not here,' she said. 'He went out an hour ago.'

She showed them Mr Hyde's rooms. Mr Utterson had seen the furniture before. It belonged to Dr Jekyll.

'My old friend must be in terrible trouble,' he said to himself.

CHAPTER 4

Who wrote the letter?

Later that day, Mr Utterson went to
Dr Jekyll's house again. Poole let him in.

'The doctor is in his laboratory,' Poole
told him.

Utterson went to the back of the
house. The laboratory was full of test-tubes,
flasks and burners. A large fire was lit in
the fireplace. Dr Jekyll was sitting very
close to it. He looked cold and ill.

'Have you heard about the murder?'
asked Utterson.

'I have,' said Dr Jekyll. 'It was a terrible business.'

'The police think your friend, Hyde, did it,' said Utterson.

'He is not my friend,' said Dr Jekyll.

'Then why has he a key to your back door? Why does he come here?' said Utterson.

'He will never come here again. He has gone away forever,' Dr Jekyll said. 'He sent me a letter saying so.'

Dr Jekyll opened a drawer and took out the letter. He handed it to Mr Utterson.

'Please read this letter and keep it,' said Dr Jekyll. 'We will never hear of Edward Hyde again. The police can stop looking.'

That night, Utterson sat by his fire, staring at Hyde's letter. He had noticed something strange.

He took out Dr Jekyll's will and he checked where Dr Jekyll had signed it. Then he looked again at the writing in Hyde's letter.

Dr Jekyll's writing was smooth and flowing. Hyde's writing was much harder to read, but some of the letters looked just the same. Had Dr Jekyll written it himself?

The idea was silly. Yet the more Utterson looked at the letter, the more he was sure. Dr Jekyll had written this letter which he said was from Edward Hyde. Why?

CHAPTER 5

The death of Dr Lanyon

The police did not find Mr Hyde.

Dr Jekyll was much happier again. He held a dinner party. Mr Utterson went and so did Dr Lanyon. They all had a good time together.

But soon afterwards, Dr Jekyll shut himself away again. Poole would not let anyone in the house. 'Dr Jekyll orders it,' he said.

Mr Utterson wondered if Dr Lanyon knew why. But when he called to see him, he was shocked. Dr Lanyon looked very ill.

'What is the matter?' cried Utterson.

'I have had a shock,' said Dr Lanyon.
'I saw something terrible and impossible.
It will kill me. I will not see or talk about
Jekyll again.'

A week later, Dr Lanyon was dead.
He left a sealed envelope. On it was written,
FOR MR UTTERSON ONLY. Inside was
another envelope. It was marked
ONLY OPEN THIS IF JEKYLL
DISAPPEARS. Utterson was worried.
What did this mean?

He was very upset. One of his best
friends was dead. The other had shut
himself away. The only person he could
turn to was his cousin, Richard Enfield.

CHAPTER 6

The face at the window

Some time later, Mr Utterson and Richard Enfield took another walk together. They passed by the door where Richard first saw Hyde.

'So that is Dr Jekyll's back door,' said Richard.

'Yes. Let's go into his courtyard,' said Utterson. 'I would be pleased to see him.'

In the courtyard, a window opened. Dr Jekyll looked out. He was pale and ill.

'Come down and join us,' shouted Richard.

Dr Jekyll replied, 'I would like to, but...'

Suddenly, his face changed. It twisted and shook. He looked a different person. He slammed the window shut.

Mr Utterson knew he had to find out what Dr Jekyll's trouble was at once.

CHAPTER 7

Dr Jekyll's letter

When he came home, Mr Utterson opened the envelope from Dr Lanyon. Inside, was a long letter. In it, Dr Jekyll told his story.

I always wanted to be a doctor. I wanted to make new discoveries about human beings.

I thought about my own character. Most of the time I wanted to do good, but not always. I felt as if there were two people inside me. One person was good, the other was evil.

I wondered if I could separate the two. I studied this for many years.

At last, I thought I had the answer. I made a secret mixture of chemicals and salts. I put them in a glass and stirred them. The mixture bubbled and I asked myself if I dared drink it.

Trembling, I lifted the glass and drank...

There was a loud knocking on the door. Someone shouted. 'Mr Utterson! Terrible things are going on at Dr Jekyll's house. Come quickly!'

Utterson put down the letter. He opened the door. Poole stood there. 'There's not a moment to lose,' he said.

CHAPTER 8

The horror in Dr Jekyll's house

They ran to Dr Jekyll's house.

'The laboratory is locked,' said Poole. 'There's someone in there. I think he's going to murder Dr Jekyll.'

There was a loud scream from inside. 'No! No!' It was a cry of pain and terror.

'This has gone on for three days,' said Poole. 'He won't let us in to help.'

Mr Utterson hammered on the door. 'Let me help you.'

Hyde's voice answered. 'Go away, you fool.'

'We must break the door down,' said Utterson. Poole fetched axes. They struck at the door. It began to give way.

'Keep out or you will see things which will drive you mad,' Hyde's voice called.

The door fell open. Hyde stood there.

'I told you to stay out,' he snarled. 'Now you'll drop dead with shock.'

On the bench were two glasses. One was empty. The other was full of a foaming liquid. Hyde picked it up and drank.

Hyde screamed with pain. His face twisted. It changed shape before their eyes. Mr Utterson could not believe what he saw. There stood his old friend, Dr Jekyll.

'This is the horror I live with,' said Jekyll. 'Who am I? Am I Jekyll? Am I Hyde? I don't know any more. When I drink my mixture, I change into Hyde. When I drink it again, I turn back into Jekyll. When I am Hyde, I do evil things. When I am Jekyll, I do good.'

'I thought I could change from Jekyll to Hyde whenever I wanted to. It was wonderful to have two lives. But one evening I went to bed as Jekyll. When I woke up, I felt different. I looked at my hand. It was hairy. I had changed into Hyde in the night. I had lost control.

'I was doing terrible things. One night, I nearly killed a little girl. Another night, I met Sir Danvers Carew. He was my friend. But as Hyde, I hated him. I smashed his face in with a stick. What can I do? I am finished.'

'Don't worry,' said Utterson. 'You are Jekyll now. Never drink your mixture again.'

'I wish it was so easy,' said Dr Jekyll.

CHAPTER 9

The only way out

Dr Jekyll suddenly clutched at his throat.

'It's happening again,' he cried.

Mr Utterson saw black hairs sprouting on the backs of Dr Jekyll's hands. More hair appeared on his face. His teeth became sharp.

'Hyde takes me over whenever he wants to. He doesn't need my mixture any more. There's no escape,' screamed Dr Jekyll.

He doubled up with pain.

'Courage, my friend,' cried Utterson. 'Fight him all you can.'

The face was now Hyde's, but the voice was still Dr Jekyll's. 'There's only one way out,' he gasped. 'I knew this day would come. I can't live any more in this terror. I am ready for death.'

'What do you mean?' said Utterson.

Dr Jekyll took a bottle from the shelf. 'This is deadly poison', he said. 'I have kept this ready'.

He poured the liquid from the bottle into the empty glass. He drank it before Utterson could stop him. In a moment, he staggered and fell. He was dead.

The two lives of Jekyll and Hyde were over.